GW00319738

I remember YARMOUTH

by

J. E. Holmes

with Dean Parkin

Rushmere
Publishing

Acknowledgements

I would like to thank Colin Tooke, for kindly allowing me to use his photographs, Dean Parkin, for all his help, and Christine Johnson for proof-reading the manuscript.

A special word of thanks must go to Ken Burton, who gave me the pick of his photograph collection, and without whom, this book could never have been published.

The photographs in this book are from the Ken Burton Collection with the exception of the following:
Jim Holmes – pages 9, 12, 21 (top), 22, 33, 63, 74, 89, 90
Colin Tooke – pages 27, 34, 38, 40, 41, 43, 44, 45, 46, 48, 50.

Excerpt from peom on page 5 taken from 'I Remember, I Remember' by Thomas Hood.

POSTSCRIPT
Ken Burton is a long-term rail enthusiast who is currently the President of the Midland & Great Northern Circle and a member of the Railway Development Society. It was in pursuit of this railway memorabilia all over the country that the majority of these Yarmouth postcards came into his possession, often purchased as part of a 'job lot' with M. & G.N. items. It is rather ironic that postcards are easier to locate at their postal destinations than at their point of purchase!

I remember
YARMOUTH
by

J. E. Holmes
with Dean Parkin

Copyright © 1995 Rushmere Publishing

All rights reserved. No part of this publication may be reproduced, stored
in a retrieval system, or transmitted in any form or by any means,
electronic, mechanical, photocopying, recording or otherwise, without
the prior permission of the publisher.

CONDITIONS OF SALE
This book is sold subject to the condition that it shall not, by way of trade
or otherwise, be lent, re-sold, hired out, or otherwise circulated, without
the publishers' prior consent, in any form of binding or cover other than
that in which it is published and without a similar condition including this
condition being imposed on the subsequent purchaser.

First published 1995 by Rushmere Publishing
32 Rushmere Road, Carlton Colville, Lowestoft, Suffolk

Typeset by Chemtech Graphics
Sussex Road, Gorleston, Great Yarmouth, Norfolk

Printed in England by Blackwell Print
133 South Quay, Great Yarmouth, Norfolk

ISBN 1 872992 09 9

Introduction

Whenever we recall memories, we mostly remember happy times and "the good old days". The sun always seemed to shine, the beach and sea were inviting and everyone seemed so nice and happy. Ice cream was a ha'penny a cornet or a penny a wafer, chocolate and toffee a penny a bar and sweets tuppence a quarter pound!

My memories here cover the years between the wars, happy years but difficult times of decay and depression, unemployment, slump which was the ruin for many firms and individuals in Yarmouth. Things became increasingly difficult as the years passed but as small children we little understood this at first.

Sadly Yarmouth and Gorleston have suffered greatly from recessions and although both make desperate efforts to meet the demands of the time, regretfully neither are as attractive as they were years ago as there is just not enough money available.

Over the years there have been many changes to the town and as I look around today it saddens me to see the decline in standards. The public gardens, although excellent in some areas, generally look neglected and the sea-front looks flashy, cheap and nasty, compared with the Old Wellington Pier Gardens and the Water Gardens on North Drive. The present Marina, built in 1979, is an eyesore and a flop. It was designed to make good the deficiencies of the old Marina, so popular in the days of Neville Bishop but handicapped by being an open-air venue. The present structure was supposed to offer every possible attraction under cover all the year around and though it was a good idea it was in the wrong place and it has failed to attract sufficient support, especially in the winter.

My heart sinks when I look at Britannia Terrace, the former Queen's Hotel, the Windmill, the Empire and the former Royal Aquarium. The Jetty and the piers all look tawdry. The Britannia Pavilion in particular is a horror, looking to me something

1

THE MARINA AND PROMENADE. GT. YARMOUTH

*(Top) The old Marina. Popular, but open to cold winds and wet weather,
whereas the modern Marina (below) has been a flop.*

like a warehouse or small factory on a pier. Though the Wellington is just about worn out it at least looks good and now that new interests are stirring, this may herald a new era for the old place. Another great help to the town would have been, in my opinion, if the money lavished on the Market Place had been spent instead on the seafront, making Great Yarmouth more attractive to visitors.

This is all in stark contrast to the Great Yarmouth of my youth. The town seemed a wonderfully attractive place and in this book I invite you to join me on visits and shopping expeditions through the town much of which has changed or long since vanished. In those days there were steam trains arriving at three stations, sailing ships and steam vessels, the quays and timber yard were piled high, there were still trams and horse drawn cars and carriages, motor vehicles were just beginning to take over, aeroplanes, airships - so much to interest small boys. Then there was always the beach, packed at holiday times, and the undeveloped Denes north and south, wonderful natural playgrounds.

Maybe like most old people I look back through rosy spectacles but for me, the intervening years have destroyed the old Great Yarmouth I enjoyed.

J.E. Holmes
August 1995

Central Beach, Great Yarmouth showing the Queen's Hotel and Britannia Terrace where I was born in 1914, just before the First World War.

4

The Home Front

I remember, I remember
The house where I was born
The little window where the sun
Came peeping in at dawn

I WAS BORN
HERE

On the Jetty, Gt. Yarmouth

I used to accompany grandfather for walks along the sea-front and sometimes we would take a stroll on the jetty. People were happy just to do that in those days, to take in the bracing sea-air. This picture shows the jetty in Yarmouth before 1914.

In my case I was born in Britannia Terrace, Great Yarmouth, within sight and sound of the sea, very right and proper for a descendent of generations of seafarers. After the 1914-18 War we lived at St. Olaves and came by train to Yarmouth for shopping, business and visits to aunts, uncles and our grandparents.

Accompanying my grandfather on his walks along the sea-front at Yarmouth was a rather dignified affair. He had been a captain on the China tea-clippers until steam ships monopolised the trade but still traded out East while freights were profitable for sailing ships. After that he went into steam ships until he retired. As a Yarmouth man he always favoured Yarmouth or Norfolk men in his crew and many old sailors sitting along the front remembered him and saluted him as captain. It was like a royal procession! Grandfather wasn't among the famous racers but made good time and safe passages. He carried a lump on the back of his head, a souvenir of the fighting in the Boxer rebellion in China when the Boxer forces entered Peking and besieged the foreign legislations. The Manchu Dowager Empress Tz'u Hsi joined them and declared war against foreign powers. Western relief forces took Tientsin by assault, set out for Peking, lifted the siege and took Peking which they burned and looted.

My grandfather was a fair but tough old character and my grandmother, originally born near Abergavenny in Wales, had her hands full bringing up a large family whilst he was away at sea. She had a wonderful managing capacity and business sense. In those days even captains had low wages and it was quite a struggle to maintain home and a growing family on his money alone so Grannie decided to go into the holiday business at Yarmouth.

In the the second half of the nineteenth century, when holidays to the coast became popular, important and wealthy families spent much time in Yarmouth. Indeed, Grandma Holmes made such an impression on one noble lady that she instructed her local banker to give Mrs Holmes every consideration and assistance required in her enterprises and she would stand by her. Such was Grannie's success that over a period of time she was able to buy the *Cromwell Hotel* and set up her family in boarding houses of their own or careers in various professions. This was a very remarkable achievement and she was respected and liked by all who knew her.

The *Cromwell Hotel* was a family and commercial temperance establishment, catering for visitors and commercial travellers. My grandmother acquired the premises in 1898 and when she died in 1919, from the after-effects of the terrible 'flu epidemic of 1918, my Aunt Helen carried it on with her husband Frank Wolsey. In those days much of the original timber and panelling in the old building survived and was really very fine. My grannie made several additions and improvements to the hotel and by the time she passed on it was quite a substantial business.

The Cromwell Hotel (below) situated on Hall Quay which my grandmother owned and ran from 1898 until her death in 1919. One of my earliest recollections is of sheltering in the old building's large cellars during the shelling of Yarmouth by the German warships in 1916. I crept upstairs and asked my Aunt Maria, "Are they gone?"

The old hotel had quite a history and there was believed to have been a tunnel underneath it that ran to the river's edge, a suggested connection with smuggling. The hotel even had its own ghost story. It was said that a group of men arrived at the hotel to discuss a plot that would result in the execution of Charles I. Unfortunately, one poor fellow did not agree to the plan and was murdered and it is told that his ghost haunts the building. In the cellar we were even shown a large dark red stain said to be blood from the body! The logical explanation for these tales is that the red stain resulted from leaking or spilt red wine, and the tunnel was most likely a large drain to get water away quickly. They are nice stories though.

During the First World War various officers were billeted to the *Cromwell,* and my brother and I were great favourites. A Major Weston used to put us through our drill. At the conclusion he would say, "Now salute the King," at which we would stand to attention and give a smart salute. Then he would say, "Salute the Kaiser," at which we would put our fingers to our noses and twiddle them contemptuously. We were made much of and were given presents of tin soldiers, guns, gun-carriages and wagons. We had a real miniature army!

Outside the *Cromwell* was a horse cab-rank and shelter and on the corner by the Post Office and Town Hall stood our war trophies, a large horned mine, a naval gun and a tank. It's a pity the army didn't learn a lesson from that tank as they soon relapsed into the horse and bayonet age. All "bull" and blanco.

The old house was originally a two-storey building and was known as the Stone House. Later, two mock Tudor storeys were added by a Mr. Goate. In 1932 the original *Star Hotel* was demolished, to make way for a new telephone exchange and my Aunt decided to sell the *Cromwell Hotel.* Once she had sold it it took the name of the recently demolished *Star Hotel* and the *Cromwell* was no more.

The original *Star Hotel* was quite a famous inn and was associated with Lord Nelson. The finest room was known as the Nelson room and was beautifully panelled, had a wonderful plaster ceiling and an outstanding fireplace. It was one of the glories of Yarmouth and an eternal disgrace upon the authorities and leading figures that it was not preserved in the town. Fortunately the Americans, realising its unique qualities acquired it and were able to reassemble it in the Metropolitan Museum in New York. God bless America!

Town Hall and Quay, Gt. Yarmouth.

The Town Hall and Quay at Great Yarmouth in the mid-1920s with the Cromwell Hotel on the left. In front of the hotel can be seen the cabman's shelter and public lavatories while I believe the top of the town's tank, one of the Yarmouth's 'trophies' from the First World War, can be seen just protruding from one of the small buildings in front of the hotel.

It seems strange that only one motor vehicle can be seen here in an area that today is besieged by cars.

Old Yarmouth was very much in evidence in my youth. The Conge, Rainbow Square and Laughing Image Corner, Middlegate, Howard Street, George Street and Fuller's Hill were overcrowded and very old. The Rows were still lived in then and with frequent fogs and poor lighting they had a rather dark and spooky atmosphere where the imagination conjured up pictures of mystery and adventure. However gloomy and badly lit there was no fear or anxiety. Everyone was safe, young or old, most doors went unlocked and cars, cycles and other property could be safely left unattended hours or even days. Consideration and respect for others made a neighbourly feeling all round.

There were few social services then. People helped themselves and their neighbours, and were proud of their independence. Workhouses were still dotted round the countryside and in this area could be found at Yarmouth, Rollesby, Oulton, Heckingham and Lingwood. One feature of the bad old days was the unhappy procession of the unemployed from the worst hit areas walking from workhouse to workhouse seeking work. Whole families passed through, their pathetic belongings piled on a pram or hand cart, with often a baby and a child or two dragging along. Most ordinary people were hard up themselves but helped as best they could, the poor helping the poor. There were also tramps, many of whom lived rough and only used the workhouse from necessity. Some were very remarkable independent characters who through some mischance or the dreadful economic circumstances of the time had lost everything. Others were not so worthy of sympathy and could be dirty, nasty people but whoever or whatever they were, it was a terrible reflection on a still wealthy and great country.

The hospital in those days depended on voluntary contributions. The food was basic and relations were encouraged to bring in extras for the patients. One great event in aid of the hospital was the Carnival. One year my cousin, Ailsa Woodger was Carnival Queen and really looked the part. We all crowded onto the balcony of Auntie Bessie's overlooking the Drive and threw paper streamers and cheered the procession. Another supporting event was 'Egg Week' which took place at the time of year when people had more eggs than they knew what to do with. Thousands were given to the hospital who 'put them down' in very large earthenware jars glazed inside and filled with isinglass (a gelatine made from fish bladders) to preserve them for use when eggs were scarce and dear. Intensive all-year production was unknown then and everyone did this to ensure a steady supply in times of scarcity. Thrift and forethought was general at that time, "Waste not, want not," being a popular saying.

In the years after the 1914-18 War it was a sad but common sight to see ex-servicemen selling all sorts of odds and ends on the streets, even singing, trying to make ends meet. Ragged and bare-footed children were not uncommon and there was much sympathy for them. It was a national disgrace after the so-called victory.

The after-effects of the First World War were still very apparent all through my childhood. I remember seeing the R33 airship pass over and during the 1914 war we often saw "Pulham Pigs" from Pulham airfield, smaller airships, and later, around 1938, I saw the German Graf Zeppelin, which was believed to have been spying, pass over the town. In the 1920s there were still extensive defences and emplacements on the dunes which were originally built for the artillery battery that protected Yarmouth Roads, much used for ships' passage or anchorage. They were deserted but still surrounded by rusty, dangerous barbed wire. In those days there were just sandy dunes until reaching Caister. No race course, no Newtown as we know it today, just open Denes over which we roamed at will. At that time the race course was still on the South Denes where there were also slipways and the remains of the famous Royal Naval Air Service installations. We were not allowed there during the 1914-18 War but I just remember the E-type small submarines in the harbour and the small naval vessels. One E submarine was lost north of Yarmouth and still lies on the sea bottom.

For many years after the war Armistice Day was strictly observed. At 11 o'clock, all traffic stopped for two minutes silence. Almost every family had lost some-one and many carried wounds bodily or mentally. It brought back such tragic memories. Gradually the memories faded and with traffic growing so rapidly it was only sensible to observe the silence and remembrance in churches and at War Memorials. My Uncle Arthur Holmes' name is on Yarmouth memorial. He was a captain in the Indian Army and was badly gassed. He lingered until 1923 but eventually died of his wounds. He was a very fine man and was sadly missed.

Gt. Yarmouth. *Blackfriars Tower.*

Blackfriars or the south-east tower which once formed part of the town's old fortifications. Over the years houses were gradually built around it but when they were demolished sometime after the Second World War the ancient town wall was revealed still intact!

The Toll House is the oldest building in the town. It was once the seat of government for the Borough of Great Yarmouth. A council chamber and court for six centuries its dungeons were used as a prison until 1879. During the Second World War the Toll House was reduced to ruins in a bombing raid and many of the town's treasures were lost. After the war it was rebuilt with the crest, salvaged from the fire and restored, proudly on the front of the building.

Kittywitches Row, No. 95, the narrowest Row in Yarmouth. Most of these Rows were still lit by gas lamps in my youth and I can even remember the gas lighter doing his rounds, pushing his pole up into the lamp and lighting the gas. In the winter the smoke from coal fires and frequent fogs and poor lighting gave the old areas a rather dark and gloomy atmosphere. Kittywitches Row in particular was very spooky and we tended to avoid it.

To those with good incomes this was a wonderful time. Everything was so cheap, a penny went a long way, a shilling was opulence and a pound a fortune. You could buy a pennyworth of chips on the market, tea was a penny a cup, cakes a penny each or seven for sixpence and what a choice! There was chocolate for a penny, tuppence or sixpence (four ounces) and Woodbine cigarettes were ten for fourpence, Players' ten for sixpence or eleven pence - ha'penny for twenty. Beer was fourpence a pint. For a haircut you might go to Ward's who were situated in King Street above a gentlemen's outfitters shop, and employed about six men. An ordinary haircut was sixpence, and I think being shaved cost tuppence. They even had a rapidly revolving brush to stimulate the hair! You could get a good dinner for a shilling or one shilling and sixpence, Hill's Restaurant in King's Street or Arnold's being great favourites. They both had three-piece orchestras and the atmosphere was very sedate. Hill's did become rather old-fashioned until Matthews took them over but Arnold's moved with the times.

As children, we had no regular pocket money but we discovered a source of income by selling blackberries at 2d a pound. My Auntie Bessie had a boarding house and gladly bought them. Further more, she introduced us to her neighbours and we were in business. My brother and I were very anxious to purchase a full cricket set but had no money. We approached Mr. Doughty and told him we proposed buying the kit piece by piece, explaining our source of income. He was more than sympathetic to our proposal and to our amazement he said, "Tell me what you want and you can pay me as you get the money." Thanks to his trust we set out to emulate Hobbs and Sutcliffe and other boyhood heroes, and helped by the abundant blackberries paid the debt off by the end of the season, an early example of what was called 'the never- never'. Mr Doughty was succeeded by his son, who was to be blinded in the 1939-45 War. He had wonderful sensitivity in his fingers though and expertly handled cameras and photographic equipment.

One activity I was not too excited about partaking in was dancing lessons which I attended at Goode's Hotel. The Goode family were well known locally, Captain Goode ran the hotel and his brother was the headmaster of Edward Worlledge School. Older local people will well remember the dancing academy presided over by Capt. Goode who was a tall, dignified and imposing M.C. Hundreds of boys

16

*The Holmes's cricket team.
Back row, left to right, Jack
Holmes, Phyllis Garwood,
Hugh Morton, me.
Sitting, Pat and Arthur
Holmes. The cricket set we
bought from Mr. Doughty
can also be seen.*

*The ballroom of Goode's Hotel, very sedate and genteel, where as a boy I was forced to attend
Captain Goode's dancing academy despite having no sense of rhythm!*

and girls attended his classes. I had to go, complete with Eton collar and a smart suit, but having no sense of rhythm I never learnt to dance! I spent my time eating the tiny iced biscuits provided, drinking lemonade and generally messing about. It's all vanished now and been replaced by amusement arcades.

A trip to the cinema, now that was a special treat, and at the Regent we could feast on dramas involving Tom Mix, Pearl White and Rin-Tin-Tin the wonder dog. Cowboys and Indians, bows and arrows, Winchester rifles and Colt revolvers all banging off and Indians biting the dust. The drama often ended with Pearl White tied head and foot to the railway line while a thundering engine complete with cow-catcher rapidly approached and a notice flashed on the screen, "To be concluded next week," all very infuriating as we seldom could attend every week.

When we came home and told my mother about these western adventures it was a dreadful experience as she would always shatter our illusions. She poured scorn

My friend, Tommy Parker, and me, in my family's pony and trap.

18

upon Buffalo Bill Cody and others whose exciting stories we loved to read and act. Mother was a daughter of the real pioneers of the Wild West and was born and brought up among the real Red Indians. Her father had been a rancher with great herds of cattle and many cowboys but no neighbours except Indians. Mother admired and greatly respected them as her parents respected and lived in peace with their Indian neighbours. Because of this, when the Indian Wars and other troubles came my grandparents and their children were perfectly safe. My mother's father and other good men held many pow-wows and maintained the peace. Troubles did arise but they were invariably due to the dishonesty, greed and arrogant attitudes of the ignorant white men. Great injustice was done to the native people and mother certainly had no time for the cowboy and Indian rubbish beloved by small boys!

The Wild West and wars excited boys in those days. I well remember from time to time, Royal Navy warships visited the town and would sit off-shore near the Yarmouth roads. It was only possible to visit them by boats and local boatmen did a roaring trade! My father and my brothers and I were fortunate to be invited to go out on the RNLI lifeboat, the *John and Mary Meiklam,* which was an extra thrill. This was in late the 1920s, later than the famous shipwreck of the vessel *Hopelyn,* whose mast stuck up out of the sea north of the Britannia Pier until around 1939. The crew were gallantly rescued by the Lowestoft motor lifeboat under Coxswain Swann and the Gorleston boat under Coxswain Fleming. It was very thrilling to sail in such a famous lifeboat!

It was also quite an exciting event when Sir Alan Cobham visited the town in 1932 with his famous flying circus during his great campaign to make Britain air-minded. The planes operated from a grassy field, where the James Paget Hospital is situated today I believe, and like many others I paid five shillings and flew over Yarmouth and Gorleston in an old AVRO two-seater fighter. It was piloted by Captain Phillips a former wartime pilot and we twice looped the loop, quite a sensation!

Another great excursion was on Easter Monday when there was a mass exodus of young people walking to Mother Brown's of Belton, or Ormesby Green. How or when this custom first began is uncertain. No-one living can say but many still remember these excursions. Mother Brown supplied lemonade and other refreshments and the children gathered wild flowers and greenery to take home. It seems to have been a tradition to get out into the 'country'. At Ormesby Green things were more organised. The local shopkeepers set out stalls which added to the many barrows of fruit, ice cream and other holiday attractions which had been trundled all the way to Ormesby. Another eagerly awaited event was the visit of 'Rububs' fair on Ormesby Green. Operated by the Underwood family the fair would then move on to Potter Heigham for the summer. Events like these were something to look forward to, and as well as annual excursions, a trip to Yarmouth by train was certainly enjoyable and memorable, helping us pull through the hard times.

BELTON GARDENS NEAR GT. YARMOUT

Another favourite trip was by horse brake to Belton Gardens. Horse brakes were something like an open air coach only bigger and were usually drawn by four horses.

Just a Line from Yarmouth

The holidaymakers loved to send a postcard home, jot down a quick note to Grandma, "hope you are feeling well, the weather's fine, had a nice walk on the pier". Of course, now these words give us a taste of the town of old from the visitors themselves and the following are just a few 'lines' from Yarmouth taken from the back of postcards . . .

Postmark: 12.30 pm, 10 August, 1914
Great Yarmouth to Lewisham
Dear Mrs Williams,
I shall be sorry when Friday comes and we have to return home. It is so interesting watching the war preparations. The trains are running anyhow – some cancelled, others running late! They say they are expecting more troops. After they are here things will be more settled.
Love S. Jackson

Postmark: 8.30 pm, 18 April, 1906
Great Yarmouth to Diss
Hope you are better. We are having lovely weather and mother is ever so much better. Can't keep away from the shrimps. This is a PPC of the Quay and the new electric trams. You would like Great Yarmouth.
from N.B.A.

Postmark: 5.30 pm, 8 August, 1933
Great Yarmouth to Blackheath, London
Dear Hilda,
Just a card to let you know we are having a good time so far. We had a full day yesterday. In the morning I went on the front then after breakfast Uncle took me down to the harbour and I found the shop where I was born. After dinner he took Arthur and I to Kessingland and Southwold in the evening. Ada's neck is burnt and I had to get some stuff for it. I don't expect Arthur will write as he is too busy getting presents.
Love Nancy

Postmark: 5.15 pm, 31 July, 1922
Great Yarmouth to Bedford
Dear Grandad,
I am having a lovely time, I paddle every day. Poor Bob has the measles and has been in house all week. I just have to keep telling him what a fine place it is! Hope you are well.
With love, Doris

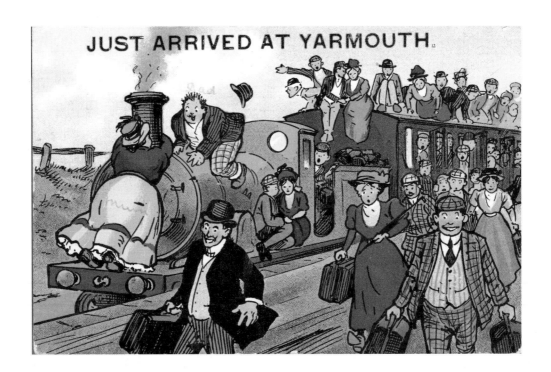

This postcard reads:

Postmark: 3 pm, 16 August, 1910
Great Yarmouth to East Dereham

Dear little Doll,

Just a postcard to let you know that I and Mum arrived at Yarmouth safe, and are feeling fine, you can pick us out on the front of the postcard. Hope you and Gladys are enjoying yourself, don't eat too many sweets. We shall be with you on Thursday and then we will take you for a drive. Writing this on the beach concert morning, give our love to Grandma and all. Love to Gladys and yourself and all.

from Mum and Dad

Just Arrived at Great Yarmouth

With my love of steam trains, Yarmouth South Town station was fascinating to me as a boy. The station, built in 1859, seemed huge with a large booking hall, waiting rooms, goods office and lamp room. There was also a porters' room and many others for staff only while the station master lived in a flat over the booking office.

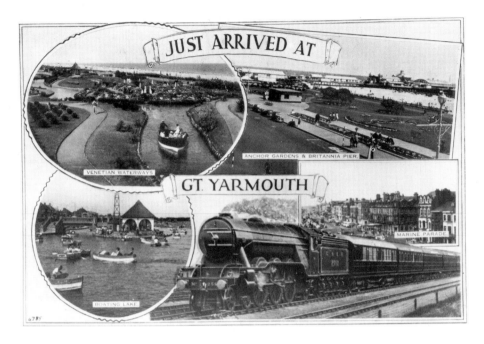

JUST ARRIVED AT

VENETIAN WATERWAYS

ANCHOR GARDENS & BRITANNIA PIER.

GT. YARMOUTH

MARINE PARADE

BOATING LAKE

Postcard showing just a few of the attractions at Yarmouth. A trip to the town was always something to look forward to, and even the journey in by train was exciting. I can remember marvelling at the powerful steam trains, they really were a sight to behold.

Just Arrived at Great Yarmouth

Visiting Yarmouth by steam train was among the highlights of our lives in the 1920s. Small boys in those days longed to be engine drivers. Such power, such speed, all so wonderful. The country stations were a sight to be seen, everything well painted, clean, tidy and all "Sir Garnet" as they used to say. Rambler roses were trained for show, flowers flourished everywhere and the grass verges were well-trimmed. Brass lamps and brasswork shone and the stationmaster was a sight to behold, not unlike an Admiral of the Fleet, with his gold braid and immaculate frock coat. There was great competition along the line to outshine all other stations.

Leaving St. Olaves we passed over Belton Common and its fringe of trees, the old firing-range and the prehistoric mounds. The train faced a long uphill climb once we were through Belton. The steam, the smoke and the sparks billowed past the windows and you could feel the terrific power of the steam engine under full throttle. At about this stage we were looking out for an iron hut occupied by an old woman with dozens of cats which were usually very much in evidence. As the engine topped the slope the driver eased the throttle and we began the long slide down to Southtown Station passing under the railway line connecting Yarmouth Beach Station with Lowestoft via Gorleston, Hopton and Corton. There was also a loop line from Southtown to connect for Lowestoft.

To small boys Southtown railway yard seemed enormous and was fascinating, all those sidings, trucks, engines, carriages and wagons. On the right stood the engine shed with an engine lifted off its wheels and bogies by the powerful lifting gear with engineers and fitters working on it. Nearby was the turn-table where the driver and fireman nonchalantly pushed the hissing monster engine round to face the return journey to London, Southtown being a terminus. How we would have liked to help with the pushing! What a network of lines, crossings, points and signals, and the water tower and coal bunkers where panting monsters watered and refuelled. Along a line of carriages passed the wheeltapper with his long hammer, activity everywhere!

The train drew into the down platform with the engine stopping just short of the station buffers at the end of the line. Nasty little boys hoped the engine would overshoot and crash into those buffers and I believe it did actually happen on one occasion due to poor brakes. Alighting from the train we would pause to admire the engine, all hot and hissing, and shyly look at our idol the engine driver, wiping his hands on some rags. I can remember Harry Moss of Ormesby in his prime and later Ivor Davis, so well known in Gorleston. Harry Moss drove for many years although towards the end of his career suffered with his legs after years of standing on the footplate. In those days the fireman and driver did not enjoy the comfortable ride - on seats - that the drivers of today have. Usually, on conclusion of a journey, ladies and gentlemen would make a point of thanking the driver for a good safe ride. The driver would reply, "Pleasure, Sir," and maybe even comment on the journey saying something like, "We were a bit late starting but I made it up after Ipswich. She went well."

At the barrier the ticket collector took up the tickets and examined the passes, the same man being there for years, while the Station Master hovered in the background, ever ready to help with enquiries. The station was huge and between the up and down platforms was a W. H. Smith & Sons book-stall with its selection of newspapers, magazines, books and sundries, a feature of most large stations. Another attraction was the slot machines offering, among other things, a penny bar of chocolate or a penny cigarette (Churchman's No.1) and a machine which punched your name on to an aluminium label. The machines were always in good working order too, and not wrecked by vandals. Trolleys laden with luggage or parcels trundled everywhere. Outside to the left of the station was a rank of horse cabs including the old-fashioned coach from the *Angel Inn* on the Market Place. This was to convey passengers and their luggage to the inn. It was mostly used by commercial travellers with their large baskets or boxes of samples. It was a very faded yellow (with *Angel Hotel* on its side) and disappeared with the advent of the motor car. The approach roads were divided by a large shrubbery and a few motor taxis were parked near the station. Later they mostly replaced the horse drawn cabs.

Southtown Road, which led to the Railway Station. St. Mary's church can be seen on the left along with many fine houses with large gardens. Over the years the well-to-do moved to the country and much of this area was given over to industry.

View of the town's market place prior to the First World War. This was one of the largest open market places in England at over three acres with hundreds of stalls from one end to the other. The majority of these were country stalls selling their own home produced goods and at that time the main suppliers to the town. Note there are no motor vehicles, only horse drawn carts and open top trams.

Shopping

Charles Bliss, 12 & 13 Broad Row. This was a fancy goods shop, typical of its day and you can see how a shop such as this would seem a real treasure house to a young boy. I don't think they could cram any more into that window!

Leaving the station and the excitement of our journey on the steam train behind us, we would perhaps head for the shops. Passing the impressively rebuilt *Two Bears* hotel, which replaced an older building in 1910, my mother often called at Drabble's the chemists on the left. It had the usual jars of coloured liquid in the window, and a large pair of scales were prominently displayed. These were for weighing babies to check their early progress as there were no clinics in those days so mothers had to rely on the chemists advice.

Further on was Mr. Francis' butchers shop with all his succulent attractions. In those days a butcher wore a straw hat and a striped apron and made a great fuss of customers. Then there was Mr. Lawn the fish merchant, whose big sash window was always open, a large marble slab inside displaying all manner of fresh fish. Nearby Castle's auction rooms always had a preview of goods for the next auction in their large windows. Castle's were also furniture removers but operated this part of the business from a repository down Southtown Road, under the name of Chateau & Co, (chateau being French for castle). The horse-drawn pantechnicons that I remember were soon replaced with motor vans. Alongside Mr. Warner's butcher shop was Mrs. Pearce's tobacconist shop, staffed by two very good-looking young ladies, her daughters I believe, a great attraction to smokers!

Continuing we passed Shipleys, the veterinary surgeon, while on the other side of the road the large wooden hoarding which screened Jewson's timber shed came to an end by the wooden tram shelter. A well-known tea stall, popular among workmen, could also be found here, later belonging to Ernie Jacobs. The tram shelter (which became a bus shelter) was remarkable as it was always clean, tidy and well kept. It had wooden seats and on the wall hung a banjo-type barometer, a large wall clock and a barograph which recorded its readings on graph paper. All these were supplied and maintained by Aldred's the well known jewellers and silversmiths. Everyday the shop's manager, a Mr. King, called to check the clock, tapped the barometer, examined the barograph and recorded the reading. All these instruments were of the highest quality and quite valuable, much respected and greatly appreciated by the public and travellers.

Before we crossed the bridge, we always paused to sniff the ozone. Coming in from the country the wonderful smell of the river was very noticeable but maybe as children our noses were more sensitive. I certainly don't notice it now! The old bridge was a bit of a relic, long past its best. To raise it men used to crank it up with hand-wheels and then the ships would slip through. When it was closed there was often difficulty in getting the two halves to meet properly! Up it would go again for another try and all this time everyone would impatiently wait.

At the foot of the bridge along Hall Quay was usually a huddle of barges, among them London sailing barges, sp'rit sail barges belonging to Everards' or Goldspinks' amongst others. These sailing craft were usually crewed by a skipper with a mate or a boy, and some of the finest sailors this country ever produced traded their vessels all round our coasts, even going over the North Sea. How I envied the boy sculling their little boat around. Little did I know what a hard rough life he lived!

One great holiday attraction from Hall Quay near the Bridge was a trip on the Broads. Several river steamers offered all day trips to Wroxham, Potter Heigham and the Broads, or via Reedham to Brundall Gardens and Norwich. Another popular cruise was to the St. Olaves *Bell* via Breydon Water and on to Somerleyton *Duke's Head*. The *Bell Inn* and the *Duke's Head* especially catered for these excursions and thousands of visitors greatly enjoyed the novel surroundings. Refreshment was provided on the trip with musical accompaniment.

Facing us at the foot of the bridge was the *Duke's Head*, a fine old inn, while further to its right was Henry's Cafe, a popular meeting place for cyclists. At C.T.C. (the Cyclist Touring Club) bicycles were left along the pavements and up the side of the Row. In those days cycles and all their equipment could be left unsecured and unattended for hours or days, no-one would dream of stealing or interfering with them. Henry's also offered accommodation to travellers, particularly cyclists.

Leaving the bridge we either headed for George Street or Clowes' Stores. Old Yarmouth residents will never forget Mr. Clowes' splendid grocery shop. Remember the smell of candles? Many people still used a candlestick with its snuffer when going to bed. How we loved candied fruit with those tasty pieces of

215276.J.V.

"YARMOUTH BELLE" AT GT YARMOUTH.(9)

The 'trip on the Broads' was certainly a popular feature of the town and here we see one of the river steamers pulling alongside Hall Quay. The fine old inn, the Duke's Head, which faced us as we walked over the bridge, can be seen to right of the picture.

Clowes' shop, here pictured in 1892, was a long established Yarmouth business. Mr. Clowes certainly had a wonderful store and it had everything a grocer's shop should have with all the delicious smells associated with them. It still makes my mouth water to think of the candied fruit they sold there!

sugar, currants, raisins and the rest. Dried fruit had to be cleaned before use in those days. Dates were compressed into great blocks which were cut and sold at 2d a pound. We really enjoyed them. It all arouses delightful memories. Clowes' had other branches out in the country at Rollesby and at Martham I believe, in addition to a delivery service.

Another of my favourite stores was Aitken's the ironmongers. Mr. Aitken was a Pickwickian character, very welcoming, polite and attentive. Full of good humour with a beaming countenance he was a fat, jolly little man. His shop was low ceilinged with brightly coloured goods, flashing galvanised buckets and pails, brooms, spades, hoes, rakes and tools of every kind, coal scuttles, oil lamps and glasses, shining nails and screws; every kind of ironmongery imaginable. To a small boy this shop was like an Aladdin's cave! Sadly, this is all gone now, replaced by Stonecutters Way.

Aldred's the jewellers fine large shop was next in line, and it was the biggest and best in Yarmouth. Mr. King with his wife and children, Joy and John, lived above the premises. It was a long-established business and among the shop records there was a reference to repairing, cleaning and rectifying Lord Nelson's watches when he was at Yarmouth! The shop is no longer a jewellers but there are still traces of its existence in a doorway where it is recorded 'Aldreds 1795'.

Opposite Aldred's was Dyer's Picture Gallery, displaying many fine framed pictures including local artists such as Seago and Arnesby Brown who have since grown in fame. At that time the Dyer's also had another shop in Market Row but the family lived behind and above the first shop. We knew them well and often exchanged visits. Harry Dyer was a great musician, a local church organist and a great supporter of the arts, sadly missed.

Next was the *Mitre* public house and Mr Gooda's eating house. Usually Mr Gooda could be found outside his establishment, touting volubly for custom! Alongside this was Marks & Spencers, a treasure house to boys. I'm told this was their first shop in Yarmouth and was on the site of the 'Bijou' a fore-runner of the cinema, and the floor sloped steeply downwards, with counters on the left, right and across the end. The entrance had a fine terrazzo surface but I cannot recall its wording. I was only interested in the German clockwork toys they kept in stock. It was just after the 1914-18 war and opinion was softening towards Germany and the toys were good and cheap.

Moving up Broad Row, Platten's was on the left and always busy. My chief interest here was in the wonderful overhead system, a means of communicating with the cashier. Wires ran to all counters, the assistant put the bill and cash in a container and sent it flying down to the cash-desk. There the bill was receipted, and with the change, replaced in the container and sent flying back to the assistant. Of course, all this was very fascinating to a small boy. At sale times slogans proclaimed, "The hatchet is out," indicating a chopping of prices!

Nearby was Ebenezer Sennit's shop, where we bought ham and especially their famous meat paste, and another well patronised shop in the area was the 'Home and Colonial' grocers. On the other side of the row was Norton Bros., the

Broad Row in 1908. This was one area we always headed for when we came to Yarmouth. With its miscellany of shops it was always well worth a visit.

R. J. Blyth, tobacconists, was at Nos. 17 & 18 Broad Row and was later to become Norton's which is how I remember it. Certainly the imposing figure of the kilted Highlander was still there in my day, an early form of advertising, which is presently on show at the Toll House Museum.

tobacconists, which was a double fronted shop outside which stood a life-sized figure of a kilted Highlander in authentic colours. He had a somewhat precarious existence when the Scottish herring fleet were about to return home! The Highlander can be seen in the Toll-house Museum now, although another one of these life size figures in the town, this time a Red Indian which stood outside Pike's the tobacconist's shop, was I believe donated to a London museum.

Further up Broad Row was the clothing shop of Mr. Hart-Green and his wife, a fascinating couple but difficult when under the influence! Their rows were awful! They had a holiday bungalow at St. Olaves and Hart-Green persistently shot at rabbits and game on our land. I remember my father threatening to shoot him if he didn't stop. They were both fiery characters.

At the bottom of Market Row was Brenner's Bazaar, later to become Peacock's, now Brett's furniture shop. It was one of several local bazaars but rather lost its attraction when Woolworth's opened in 1924. Going up the Row we usually stopped at Jessie Heyhoe's fish shop, number 20. Jessie had a long association with our family and also sold my Uncle Woodger's famous kippers. Further up on the right was Turner's pastry shop and restaurant, a double fronted shop with cakes in the windows. Entering the shop we passed through beaded curtains into the restaurant. It was a very popular stopping place. As far as I remember a pot of tea with extra hot water in a jug and six cakes was a shilling with any more cakes after that costing a penny each. I believe the two-course lunch including a cup of tea was one shilling and sixpence. Almost opposite was the London Dentistry where unfortunately I had to go one Christmas Eve as there was nowhere else open and I never forgot the experience. Mother didn't want me moaning with toothache all through the festive season, so in between my sobs they pulled out my tooth for a shilling, no anaesthetic, real strong arm stuff!

The International Stores could be found at the end of Market Row and was one of many excellent grocery shops in Yarmouth. I remember Mr. Clarke their traveller who solicited orders for delivery to the country by van. The miles that man travelled and the long hours worked is unbelievable. The shop was always busy too. The cashier was at a cash desk in a cubicle on the left as you entered, next to the dry-goods counter and I was fascinated by the speed and skill of the assistants as they weighed and folded the blue bags of sugar, currants or what have you. On the opposite counter was a huge cheese deftly cut by a steel wire as required and neatly wrapped. I loved the bacon slicer as the assistant twirled the handle. It had a lovely sound in operation slicing through the bacon. As a special treat we had 'Palethorpes Cambridge Sausages' which were supposed to be extra good. They cost a shilling a pound compared with eight pence for local pork sausages and sixpence for beef sausages. However, I preferred Allen's country pork sausages from the Market but it's hard to say who's were best as all sausages were so tasty then, unlike the mysterious things we get today.

*Bretts' was situated at the bottom of
Market Row and eventually expanded
into the building on the left and now
has premises both sides of the row.
When I was a boy that shop on the left
was the home of Brenner's Bazaar
which specialised in cheaper goods. It
did seem to lose a lot of its trade to
Woolworth's which opened in 1924.*

Sayer's in Market Row was typical of tailors at this time. The window displays were immaculate and always worth a good look by shoppers. Window dressing seems a thing of the past today.

Turner's pastry shop and restaurant, here shown in 1900. This was a popular stopping place for weary shoppers and tourists to quench their thirst before returning to the bustle of the town's streets. As far as I can remember a pot of tea with extra hot water in a jug and six cakes was a shilling and extra cakes a penny each.

Turning left at the Market Place we gazed into Smith & Daniels' windows. The tool-shop's display was full of model makers' lathes and tools of every kind. They did saw-sharpening and setting and were a Mecca for model engineers and engineers in general. In this area around the Market Place were various shoe shops. Cash & Co., Turner's and Freeman, Hardy & Willis. The Plaza cinema, unkindly referred to as the "Flea Pit" had hundreds of children queued up for matinees etc. Alas, we were not allowed to attend.

Another attraction was Foulsham's Eating House, a double fronted building. In one window there was always a large ham or joint of meat for carving. It made your mouth water to see it! Inside it was divided into cubicles on either side. Not unlike such places in cowboy films, all very cosy and private. The meals on offer were all

from fresh home-grown produce. The steak and kidney pie swam in wonderful gravy with a lovely flaky pastry crust. It was the real McCoy. Desserts included such delights as jam roly poly pudding, apple pie and custard or treacle pudding, just the stuff to fill a hungry family. The roast beef and Yorkshire pudding was another mouth watering dish. Good old English fare, well cooked, all for one shilling and sixpence and they were known to ask, "Did you want any more?"

Near the church was Ceiley's the herbalist. He was a well-educated man and knew his herbs and much about nature's remedies. He was scoffed at by the then so-called 'modern' medicine but we now better appreciate the undoubted merit of plants and herbs.

Leach's the ironmongers and Norman's furniture shop in the Market Place were both and still are good old family businesses. Barnes' the grocers were also a well established business although now closed. On the corner of the Market Place stood The *Gallon Pot* then better known as 'Boroughs' as that family kept it since 1812. It was bombed during the last war, then rebuilt. On Brewery Plain stood 'The Wrestlers'. This old inn had many notable connections with the past and is featured in the famous diaries of both Parson Woodforde and Silas Neville and above all with Lord Nelson and Lady Hamilton. Next door was Porter's woodworkers' establishment displaying turned table legs, beading, veneers and everything necessary to woodworkers. The shop was a bit of a jumble inside but had a fine bow window, which was, like so many of these shops, swept away after the war and replaced by modern offices.

◄ (Facing Page)
Foulsham's dining room was situated in the Market Place and always had a large ham or joint of meat for carving displayed in one window. The food on offer was good old English fare, steak and kidney pie, roast beef and Yorkshire pudding and desserts included jam roly-poly pudding and apple pie and custard. Another mouth watering memory!

Ceiley's the herbalist was situated near St. Nicholas church. His windows were full of the strangest objects with all kinds of dried herbs and odd things in jar and bottles. It certainly attracted the eye.

A tram makes its way round the Market in Yarmouth at about the time of the First World War. Being situated at the very heart of the town, the Market Place in Yarmouth was always a hive of industry. Note Palmer's to the left of the picture, still a big department store in the town today.

MARKET PLACE GT. YARMOUTH

The Market Place before the First World War. On the right can be seen the Grand 1d Bazaar which was later to become Nichol's dining rooms, one of the finest eating houses in the town. Next to it can be seen Fish-Stall House, a well known pub.

Just a Line
from Yarmouth

Postmark: 11.30 am, 12 August, 1938
Great Yarmouth to Hemel Hempstead

Dear S.,

We are having such a good time here with wonderful sunny weather. We went round the market this morning and looked in the large 14th century church. I quite fancy a hat here.

Hope you are well,

Love Isi

Postmark: 8.30 am, 17 August, 1913
Great Yarmouth to Ramsgate

Dear Mabel,

Arrived quite safely about 6.15 had a good journey, weather grand. Got nice diggins and having a lovely time on the sands. Great Yarmouth even makes Father smile! The earlier you book the better. Hope you are feeling well.

Arthur xxxxxx

Postmark: 3.30 pm, 23 July, 1928
Great Yarmouth to Wimbledon

Dear Grace,

Many thanks for the saucy card this morning. Have been for a wash in the briny with D. Leach this morning. It was lovely. I see there is still plenty of fish here yet!

Love from all, Horace

Postmark: 11.15 am, 19 Sep, 1930
Great Yarmouth to Dewsbury

Hooray the sun has come even though there is a wind. Given a days notice for a bloater for breakfast, altho. still haven't got one. The hotel is good to a point, tell you what the point is later.

Half the party seem to have been ill, perhaps it was all those bloaters for breakfast? Get me some pink pyrethrums on Saturday please. They're the only thing I can't find here! Hope you are behaving yourself.

Lily

REGENT ST GT YARMOUTH.

Pre-1914, looking up Regent Street from the Town Hall with no Post Office on the left corner. Regent Street was home to many interesting shops and among them was my Uncle Sam Woodger's retail establishment, along with Brunning Bros. shop, the outstanding nurseryman in the area.

There were many different shops in Yarmouth and many different ways to get to them. Another route from the Haven Bridge was when we turned up Regent Street and passing the Post Office, came to No. 17. This was Woodger's, a large shop from where boxes of the famous kippers were dispatched to order. On the corner of Regent Street and Howard Street was Burgess's the hairdresser and fancy goods shop while on the other side of the road was Brunning Bros., seedsmen, florists and nurseryman's shop, the outstanding business in the district. Their nursery was at Bradwell/Browston and Harry Brunning knew and loved all plants, cultivated or wild. He was a man of wide interests who was well-known and much respected.

Continuing on the left we came to Baird's the shoe shop and next to that Maddison Miles and Co, Auctioneers & Estate Agents. I remember Owen Miles, a rather handsome man, and one of the finest auctioneers and estate agents anywhere. Unfortunately, like so many auctioneers, he was a heavy drinker and that and women proved his eventual downfall. His assistant, a Mr. Sayer, loyally stayed with him right to the end though.

Before they moved to the Market Place, I seem to remember the Scotch Wool Shop situated just before you got to Arnolds Bros. store along King Street. Arnold's was a great shop and one of the largest in Yarmouth. It was burnt down in 1919 and the store's windows which once had displayed toys were reduced to a mess of rubble and I can well remember how upset I was to see this and the shop completely destroyed. Opposite Arnold's was Carr & Carr's music shop, Salmon & Gluckstein's tobacconists shop and a Freeman, Hardy and Willis shoe shop. Stone's the tailors was near the 'Mercury' office in Regent Street. In the window stood a bale of suiting, one piece draped over a chair, nothing else. It was a very superior bespoke tailors, still operating in Norwich, in those days catering for the gentry and naval and military uniforms!

In King Street opposite Arnold's was Boning's another large popular family store later replaced by Marks & Spencer. In the Market Place was Palmer's, a fine store with a high reputation for quality and service and still trading along the same lines today. Many girls trained at Palmer's in all departments and it was a recommendation to have worked there. Next to Palmer's was the *Red House* public house, later well known for Mr. Moore's miniature railway which ran around the bar. The house was later incorporated in the main store and Row 59 was blocked up. We also used to visit Cooper's the ironmongers which stood nearby.

On the other side of the Market Place was Arthur Hollis, the seedsman and corn-chandler. It was a flourishing business especially among small farmers, small-holders and poultry farms. They did not grow their own seeds but were good suppliers. I was told of a well-known local farmer who asked for Hollis's special turnip seed. The assistant scooped the required amount out of a sack marked "Finest turnip seed." "No," said the farmer, "I want the best." Mr Hollis came through and said, "Give me the scoop." He went out the back of the shop and

King Street, Great Yarmouth

King Street looking south from the end of the market with Kerridge's ironmongers shop on the left. Also shown is Arnold Bros. to the right, located on the corner of Regent Street and King Street, which was the largest store in Yarmouth.

KING STREET, GREAT YARMOUTH.

The King Street junction with Regent Road looking north. On the tram coming towards us you can see an advertisement for Billy Dawson's baking powder, which was famous in Yarmouth. This brought back memories of his other adverts which featured Billy himself and fascinated me. His picture oozed self confidence!

Note the policeman with summer helmet at junction with Regent Road.

scooped out identical seed from a sack, parcelled it, took a label and wrote "Hollis' best turnip seed." "That's right," said the farmer, "Just what I want!"

Down Market Road was the *Feather's Inn*. At one time it had a large, glass-covered entry inside which grew a fine grapevine of white grapes. Opposite the inn was Frosdick's the horse meat shop. The meat was supposedly for feeding dogs and other animals but it was said that the meat was so good, tasty and cheap that some people ate it themselves! Next door or nearby was Southey's leather and sports shop, Cooper's fire-place and stove showrooms and an eating house owned by Mr. & Mrs. Barber, who had been stalwarts of the labour movement, great fighters for social justice and democratic government in their London days. On the corner of the Market Place was the '1d Bazaar', formerly the old Blue Coat School and later to become Nichol's Dining Rooms, one of the many fine eating houses in Yarmouth. Most of the time it was packed and there were great meals.

On Theatre Plain was Botwright's, the hairdresser. During the last war I returned on leave and was thrilled to have my hair cut by his daughter, a stunning blonde, as all the male hairdressers had been called up. Facing customers was a printed sign saying, "We will not discuss the possibility of defeat." At that time things were going very badly and some faint hearts were saying we should come to terms with Hitler but not Reggie Botwright. Adjoining his shop was the Conservative Club and on the Plain, Buckle's the printer. At the other end stood the Theatre Royal, which faced north towards the Plain.

The popularity of the cinema destroyed the old theatres and this wonderful historic gem was demolished to be replaced by the Regal in 1932. I well remember the old theatre as my uncle Frank Wolsey was a shareholder and manager. If there were empty seats we were allowed in free - if it was a popular show we would be unlucky.

In 1924 F. & W. Woolworth opened their large new store at the top of Regent Road, "Nothing over 3d or 6d" emblazoned over the top in gold letters. It was a marvellous place, full of treasures, all no more than 6d which to small boys with very little money was a dream come true. My savings for Christmas amounted to about half-a-crown and what a choice there was at Woolworth's for that money! First there was a 6d glass cake-stand for mother. It was made in Czechoslovakia and looked very grand. Then there was a 6d briar pipe for Pa, a 6d swivel-top pencil box

The Feather's Inn, situated in Market Road, complete with the sign that caused me quite a bit of bother! It can be seen on the photograph showing the Prince of Wales' feathers, three ostrich feather and the motto, 'Ich Dien' which means 'I serve'. This caused me to cross swords, or rather pens, with the local historian Mr. Ecclestone, who had the sign repainted with the words "Hic Dien" which he mistakenly maintained was correct. However the brewery, Lacons, stepped in and wisely replaced it and the corrected sign is still there today.

53

for Arthur, a book for Jack and a bright toy for baby Pat. If we were lucky enough to have some money left over we would perhaps buy some toffee, broken from big slabs with a small hammer, or maybe some delicious coconut-ice, two flavours. Happy days!

At the corner of Regent Road and King Street was Tom Green, the hatters, while next door was Yallop's the photographers. We had our pictures taken there, so solemn and still. Opposite Woolworth's was Masterson's fish shop, still there today, which specialised in sending away boxes of Yarmouth bloaters, labelled "A Present from Yarmouth". There was a unique flavour to bloaters at that time and they were very popular.

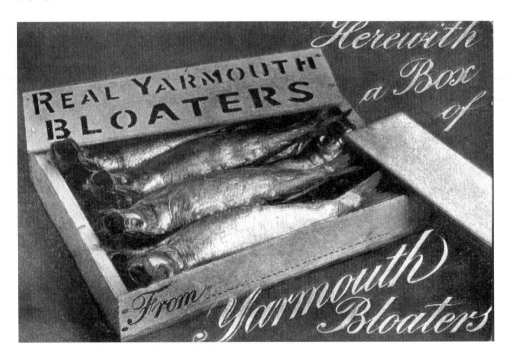

Real Yarmouth Bloaters could be sent to a friend, giving them a real taste of the seaside!

The opening of St. John's Garage on May 11th 1911.

There were many private houses on Regent Road then and few shops that really interested us, but we did notice Wiggen's baby carriages, and Mr. Willgrass's grocery, recently opened. On the right was St. John's Garage, at the time the biggest and the most important motor business in Yarmouth. In its large showrooms were displayed the gleaming models of the day, far beyond the means of most people then. Only the well-to-do could afford to own one. I remember we were very impressed that my Uncle Sam Woodger had a Sunbeam Saloon and a two seater

Regent Road in the 1920s with St. Mary's church in the background. This was the main road to the beach but as the picture shows, a different style of hat was the only concession made to summer in those days!

bull-nosed Morris Cowley with a dickey at the back, all earned from selling kippers!

Then there was another photographer's shop, Nobb's, I believe. They also sold cameras and photographic items. Next was the Regent. It had a fine stage and presented live shows but I remember it mainly as a cinema we used to attend for a special treat.

Down a passage way beside the Regent was a large stand-by oil engine with an impressive flywheel. This was used to drive the dynamos should the electricity supply fail. Nearly opposite the Regent was Mr. O. Atkinson's motorcycle shop. At first I hardly noticed this but later was fascinated by the Nortons, BSAs, Ariels, Triumphs and other well-known makes. There was a workshop in the basement to which the machines were lowered for repair. He was a great man for motor cycles in his day.

Next we liked to gaze in Doughty's sports shop. He was a great character, a Yorkshire man, I believe, who had been a gold miner in the 1898 Gold Rush in Klondike. My father too had joined the scramble for gold in the most atrocious conditions in the world but they never met.

Opposite was the Savoy on Nelson Road, a popular high-class restaurant and further down Regent Road on the left was St. Quentin's music shop. Years ago my brother Jack was sweet on Molly St. Quentin. She married an American but later returned to Yarmouth. Further down was Pownall's fishing tackle shop.

During this walk through the past I may have missed out some shops and note-worthy establishments because as a child they would not have interested me. Standards everywhere were very high and every effort was made to keep it that way. In those days of course we always addressed people as Mr., Mrs. or Miss, none of this casual sloppy Tom, Dick or Harry business. At this time many shops were open until nine at night on Saturdays and for the staff it was long hours and low pay. This was the era of family businesses, with the owner on the premises. Mr. Cooper, Mr. Palmer and Mr. Leach were always available in their establishments and any complaints were dealt with personally and the matter put right. This is the era I like to remember . . . .

The visitors certainly loved the sea and flocked to the beach. Just look at the crowds, not an inch to spare, and yet the sea itself only has a handful of paddlers. People just wanted to rest and enjoy the sea air.

Days by the Sea

3132   New Bridge and Town Hall, Gt. Yarmouth

The railway on the quayside, seen here in the foreground, was of great interest to me when I was a boy. Consisting of a train of trucks and wagons a man walked in front with a little red flag and a bell to warn pedestrians that the train was coming.

On our trips to Yarmouth in the fishing season, we always brought home fresh herring and always enjoyed lots of bloaters and kippers. We had lots of split kippers, rejects from the best at my Uncle Woodger's yard. Herrings were hawked by boys straight from the boats, some stolen we suspected. They were often sold in a 'frail', which were baskets woven from rushes, for one shilling a dozen.

A great attraction to small boys but a nuisance to pedestrians and traffic was the goods train that ran from Vauxhall Station over the river and along the North Quay past the foot of the bridge to South Quay. It consisted of a train of trucks and wagons. The engine was specially suitable for the job and had a 'cowcatcher' on the front. As it slowly proceeded along the quays the driver rang a bell and blew the whistle to warn everyone and as an extra precaution a man with a red flag walked in front of the engine. Ivor Davis of Gorleston drove it at one time and it was used as a connection between cargo ships and the railway but was never successful. Mr. Davis is now over ninety years old and still drives a car!

Of course, there was much more coastal shipping in those days with regular passage to places such as Hull, London and countries as far afield as Holland, Belgium, France and Germany. In addition to this there was a huge timber trade with Norway, Finland and Sweden, Canada and other timber exporting countries. Much of the timber from Scandinavia and Finland arrived in large three masted sailing barques and they were a great attraction along the quays or when towed into harbour. It was often a very rough voyage and the deck cargo would shift causing an alarming list. Sometimes it was too much for the crew to correct at sea and the ship would anchor off the harbour with the lower yard arms touching the water. The crew had to shift the cargo over as the Port Authorities would not allow entry in such a state as there was always the danger of capsize and blocking the harbour. Fellow's ship building yard and dry dock always seemed busy although Beeching's or any others may have closed at the time I remember.

The fisher girls on the South Denes gutting the fish in the farlings which was the sort of trough they are standing over. The girls worked in teams of three, two gutting and one putting the fish into barrels. They had to be so careful in their work because if they packed a barrel wrong it could cause a whole shipment to be sent back. With this in mind, their speed and precision was astounding.

5196 Herring Season. Gt. Yarmouth. Drifters Unloading their Catch.

Drifters unloading their catch using a quarter cran basket which was used for hoisting the fish from the hold of a vessel onto the quayside. Then the fish would be put into swills, large baskets which were only used locally and eventually replaced with metal boxes.

As a boy I used to go along the quays unhindered. Timber was piled high every-where. Jewson's, Palgrave & Brown, Orfeur & Bellin, Wenn's, Porter's and other timber importers and merchants. We walked over the entrance to Fellows' dry dock and the shipyard and slipway. There was always something interesting to see. The tall-masted barques loaded with timber from Scandinavia and Finland were romantic to view. In those days the unloading was by man power and we marvelled to see men balancing great timbers on leather pads on their shoulders and crossing gangplanks to stack the timber in piles on the quay side. The gangplanks rose and fell under the weight of man and timber. It showed wonderful balance and great strength and endurance unloading and stacking timber.

Another activity that can hardly be believed today was coaling. Most ships were coal burners, especially the herring drifters, and every hundredweight was carried on men's shoulders and shot into the bunkers. Also much other cargo entailed a lot of man-handling. It was a hard, hard life for low wages.

The port tugs were always fussily busy or lying at quays. I remember the paddle tugs, *Yare* and *United Service,* wonderfully seaworthy and active until their end, and in the summer they carried holiday makers on sea trips. Then there was the Port and Haven tug *The George Jewson* and I can remember her skipper, 'Shiner' Collins, who had been a herring drifter skipper out of Yarmouth. *The George Jewson* and *The Tactful* were screw-driven steam tugs. Old Harry who was skipper of *The Tactful* was quite a character in the real tug-boat tradition and went out in all weathers and sea conditions. There was no wheelhouse on *The Tactful,* only a raised bridge protect-ed by a low canvas dodger. She was a fine sea boat and kept busy. In later years I admired the fine Dutch deep-sea tugs, *Nordzee* and *Oostzee.* These were really large, well-equipped modern vessels capable of operating in any seas around the world.

Coastal steamers were also regular visitors to the port. Vessels such as *Yarmouth Trader, City of Malines,* the Everard motor ships, Metcalf's 'M' steamers, *Daniel M* and others. Many small coasters would even go up-river to Norwich, principally with coal. Another sight, almost forgotten, were the sp'ritsail barges, London barges as they were known, usually belonging to Everard's and Goldspink's, and last of all was Bob Roberts' privately owned *Cambria,* relying only on sails and the goodwill of local shippers.

Despite the working life of the river, the holidaymakers were never very far away. By the Town Hall river steamers were ready to carry passengers to Brush Quay at Gorleston, a most interesting trip which was a taste of the sea-air for the visitors. All summer Yarmouth was always packed with holidaymakers and between the wars among them were the 'Garri Boys'. I well remember them, a large number of very lively young men, unmarried I believe, mostly from London who spent their holiday at the Garibaldi Hotel owned by the famous Joe Powell. They were were up to all sorts of activities and full of high spirits. Fortunately Joe Powell and his wife were wonderful characters who had a great influence over them and directed their energies into all sorts of beneficial activities. Their help with the Carnival in support of Yarmouth Hospital was more than welcome.

In its heyday the Garibaldi Hotel was owned by Joe Powell and was home to the famous 'Garri Boys'. When Joe took over the premises in 1890 it was only a small public house but over the next few years the Garibaldi was converted into a four-storey hotel.

A river steamer and the United Service alongside the Town Hall and quay in the 1920s. The river steamers performed a shuttle service carrying passengers to Brush Quay at Gorleston, and were double-ended and drove either way with propellors and steering gear at both ends. To make the return journey the skipper just moved to the opposite end of the boat and off she went!

Belle Steamers at Gt. Yarmouth.

Probably taken on a busy weekend, this picture shows two Belle steamers along the quayside at Great Yarmouth. In the foreground the Southend Belle is preparing to sail whilst behind her, the Walton Belle awaits her passengers.

The Singers' Ring at Yarmouth was situated to the south of Britannia Pier and was hugely popular. Top musical acts and sometimes drama shows would come from all over the country to perform there. The Singers' Ring ceased when hostilities broke out in 1939 and after the war was forgotten.

The visitors certainly loved the sea and many small boats worked the beach, the seashore being the main attraction. Taking our bucket and spade we would walk down to the beach, packed with people enjoying the rest with the aid of sun and sand. We would make sand castles, paddle and splash about. Slatted wooden walk-ways led to the sea and at intervals the beach stalls provided refreshments, ices, soft drinks, and fancy goods. Photographers had sites where we were photographed on motor cycles or against other backgrounds. 'Punch and Judy' always drew a crowd but I was half afraid of the violent and malevolent Mr. Punch. There were beach concert-parties, and 'Nigger minstrels' on a stage enclosed by temporary fencing, and the famous 'Singers' Ring', a popular beach attraction everyone visited. Then there were trips to Scroby Sands.

In those days regulations were not so strict and shrimps were sold to tourists and locals alike on the street by ladies with nice clean pinafores and sun bonnets. They used to sit by the pavements with big baskets full of brown and pink shrimps and sold them by the pint in paper bags. Home-made ice cream was also sold from small barrows holding a container of ice cream, a glass fronted box of wafers and cornets and a measure for serving. Some of it was very yellow and varied greatly but most was good and wholesome. There were also many local sweetmakers with premises in the Rows such as 'Big Jim' Thompson whose descendants are still trading on the market. Docwra's, the big rock-makers down Regent Road were there even then and it was fascinating to watch the making of Yarmouth rock. They also made and sold sweets from a shop in Middlegate and very good they were too.

Yarmouth had many attractions for the holidaymaker and we locals would enjoy them too. There were many different and diverse things a child could do with his time. The 'jockey' scales with the highly polished brass weights were great fun for onlookers. With great glee they made a show of weighing the fattest people who could be induced to be weighed, pretending the scales would collapse or that there were not enough weights! The sand artist was also very popular with his really life-like scenes erected out of moist sand. This was just after the 1914-18 war and a typical scene was of a stricken gun team, the dying horse and its rider. This and other heart-rending scenes were real tear-jerkers. It brought back the war and all its tragic consequences.

The Yarmouth Hippodrome was an outstanding venue and was one of only three arenas specially built in this country to stage circus exhibitions, which it is shown advertising in the photograph. I can well remember the animal acts of all kinds, clowns, trapeze and high wire acts which scared me every time!

◀ (Facing Page)

The Central Cinema opened on 5th April 1915. However by the early 1920s the name had changed to the Plaza although we knew it as the 'fleapit'.

During my childhood the cinemas came to prominence and soon became very popular. It was usual to queue patiently for admittance to the more popular films. There was the main film and the 'B' film and the Pathé News plus the British news features. The news films were far superior in film quality and content to the present television news. The cinemas were warm and comfortable and seats were priced from 4d to 1/3d (approximately two pence to six pence in today's money, of course worth a lot more in those days!) The Regent, the Empire, the Aquarium and the Gem vied for custom in the main holiday area along with others already mentioned. One outstanding venue was the Hippodrome, specially built by Mr. Gilbert in 1903 to stage circus exhibitions. It is one of only three built in this country for the circus and presented some wonderful shows. Animal acts of all kinds, clowns, trapeze, and high wire acts that scared me every time. Often the circus ring was filled with water and we were treated to aquatic displays featuring seals, walrus and other delights including mermaids. How we admired the magnificent ringmaster and brave lion tamer with his cracking whip, not to mention the beautiful horseriders and other delights.

The Britannia Pier had a splendid pavilion staging many popular shows. The pier has had a very chequered history. Three times it was burnt down, the 1914 occasion being attributed to suffragettes. Twice it was cut in two by ships coming adrift in severe storms but like the Phoenix it rose from the ashes. Its best times were during Mr. Nightingale's ownership. Personally I feel the present pavilion is a blot on the landscape; to me it looks like a factory on a pier. Maybe history will repeat itself! The Barfield Brothers ran the pier very successfully in the 1930s and also ran very popular sea trips in their ship *The Brit* from Town Hall Quay.

To the north of the pier was the memorable Revolving Tower. Standing at around a hundred and twenty-five feet tall, the tower had a cage which ascended and also revolved, giving marvellous views of the sea and countryside. It was lifted by a steam engine with cables and revolved by an electric motor which was rather erratic!

The gardens opposite Britannia Terrace were very formal, enclosed by metal hoops and with notices saying, "Keep off the grass." Nearby was the Royal Aquarium seating around 2000 people and possessing the largest stage in East Anglia. It was another of Mr. Nightingale ventures. He also owned the Queen's Hotel, unquestionably the premier hotel in Yarmouth, situated at the other end of Regent Road, fronting on to Marine Parade. Mr. Nightingale attracted the leading London shows to his Royal Aquarium including the famous D'Oyly Carte with the Gilbert & Sullivan masterpieces. Its name became 'Royal' through the patronage of the Prince of Wales, later Edward VII and 'Aquarium' was derived from the many large glass tanks exhibiting a great variety of exotic fish and other marine life. We knew Mr. Nightingale's son Walter and his wife and their daughter Valerie as they had a bungalow at St. Olaves. Mr. Walter Nightingale was always very dapper with a morning coat, striped trousers, spats and a button hole.

In the mid-1950s Britannia Pier was restored and its theatre re-opened in time for the 1958 season. A modern structure, I feel this new pavilion is a blot on the landscape and compared with its predecessors looks like a factory on a pier!

The original Britannia Pier opened in 1858 and within twelve months the pier had been short-ened by 80 feet after a ship collided with it, which happened again ten years later, resulting in 100 feet being lost. In 1902 the pier was replaced with a new structure and the ornate pavilion in the photograph was erected by Boulton & Paul of Norwich though it was totally destroyed by fire in 1909.

Britannia Pier, Gt. Yarmouth.

The second pavilion was not quite as elaborate in design when it was built to replace the one that burned down in 1909. However, on April 14th 1914 the pavilion was burnt down again, the fire allegedly started by suffragettes.

Rebuilt again, the pavilion was later enlarged with a ballroom being added in 1928 and was visited by the Duke and Duchess of York in 1931. Within a year though the fire jinx had struck again when, on the 3rd August 1932, the pavilion met with the same fate as its predecessors.

In 1939 the pier was halved again, this time not by accident but for safety as it was considered that it could aid an enemy invasion attempt.

BRITANNIA PIER, GT. YARMOUTH.

6080   BRITTANIA PIER, GREAT YARMOUTH.

The fourth pavilion, pictured here after 1945, had other attractions added such as a ballroom and restaurant, amusements and children's rides. Since the war top names such as Frankie Howerd, Max Bygraves, Ronnie Ronalde and Norman Evans were among the top names who had spent their summer on the Pier, and on the picture a show is advertised featuring comedians Jimmy Jewel and Ben Warris and also an up and coming young singer by the name of Anne Shelton. Ted Ray had been booked for July 1954 when on 20th April 1954 fire broke out again and this time ravaged the whole pier and the pavilion was destroyed again.

76

T.S.M.V.

'BRIT'

BRITANNIA

:: PIER ::

Great Yarmouth

Sea trips on 'The Brit' became quite an attraction and a regular service was run from the Town Hall to the Britannia Pier to give holidaymakers and locals alike a taste of sea-air and life on the waves.

◀ (Facing Page)

The Revolving Tower was a memorable feature of the town in my youth and was built in 1897 and stood tall at 125 feet. Visitors entered a cage which slowly revolved whilst ascending to the top giving a marvellous all-round view of Great Yarmouth. The tower met its demise during the Second World War when it was dismantled and used for scrap.

Obviously this postcard caption writer had never been to Great Yarmouth and presumed that this must be a view from an aeroplane. This was of course not the case and was in fact taken from the Revolving Tower, showing the beach and part of Britannia Pier around the time of the First World War. What a view for 3d!

The Royal Aquarium, just after the First World War. Seating around 2000 people and possessing the largest stage in East Anglia, the theatre was another of Mr. Nightingale's business ventures and he succeeded in bringing top notch shows to the town giving Yarmouth the chance to see the latest West End productions.

Marine Parade and Aquarium, Great Yarmouth.

Marine Parade and Aquarium, seen far right, in a more sedate and genteel era around the time of the First World War. Note the fruit barrow in the foreground and behind him another man with a barrow selling Yarmouth rock.

MARINE PARADE AND WELLINGTON PIER, GT. YARMOUTH.

64

A view of Marine Parade in the 1920s, with the swimming pool on the left, and the jetty and Wellington Pier in the distance. To the right in the foreground of the picture can be seen the jockey scales where you could be weighed to the amusement of onlookers.

The open-air swimming pool, unheated in the 1920s. It was quite popular in the summer but seemed freezing even in the sunshine. It was always very cold with that east wind!

Promenade, Pier & Sands, Gt. Yarmouth

Another view of Marine Parade and the Promenade, dating back to the 1920s. At the entrance to the jetty, on the right, were two cannons dating back to the time of the Battle of Sebastapol.

(Facing Page) ▶

The South Beach with Wellington Pier in the distance.

South Beach, Gt Yarmouth

Wellington Gardens, G' Yarm

INTERIOR WINTER GARDENS, GT YARMOUTH.

The interior of the Winter Gardens in the 1920s was a sight to behold. Roller skating can be seen here, and this was indeed a popular activity. On other occasions other events were staged there such as exhibitions and shows.

◀ (Facing Page)

I have fond memories of Wellington Gardens and for me this picture evokes the sedate and refined atmosphere of the era.

An early picture of the Pleasure Beach. The origins of the town's Pleasure Beach date back to the late nineteenth century when a 'switchback' was erected on the North Denes which later developed into a scenic railway. This was replaced in 1912 with a railway of a superior design and construction but that was destroyed by fire along with other rides and attractions in 1919. This allowed for the complete redevelopment of the area and subsequently an amusement park was laid out. In 1932 a Mountain Ride was introduced which was the forerunner of many similar rides.

Just a Line from Yarmouth

Postmark: 6.30 pm, 9 August, 1909
Great Yarmouth to London

Dear Father,

I am writing this at Gorleston. Mother and myself came by steamer and we both enjoyed it very much. I went with Donald and saw the large London boat by the side of the quay. Crowds of people around it, the whole town is full.

From Violet

Postmark: 11.15 am, 9 August, 1921
Great Yarmouth to Sheffield

Gran and Granddad,

Just a line from Yarmouth. I am writing for the last time on the sands. Returning Saturday & will be home about 4. Still having very bad weather but with all that must say I am having a jolly time. Children just do not want to come home. Just suits us to watch the boats.

From William & Marjorie

Postmark: 6.30 pm, 22 July, 1924
Great Yarmouth to Halifax

Dear George,

What-Ho! We have just been on the jetty and are now sitting in the gardens enjoying the breeze. Been up the tower like you said. It's the top of the world isn't it? Having a grand time.

Love Nellie

Postmark: 8 pm, 24 July, 1935
Great Yarmouth to Worksop

Dear John,

You will see I have been to the seaside. We had a very good time but coming home Saturday. Been on a mountain ride at the beach. Yes, it is Yarmouth! We are all well, hope you are too.

With love, May

The Prince of Wales often visited Yarmouth accompanied by Lily Langtry and other ladies. On one occasion he inspected the local military volunteers staying at Shadingfield Lodge, now a well known hotel, opposite the Wellington Pier which in those days along with the Winter Gardens was at its peak. The gardens with the bandstand in the middle were tasteful and genteel and representative of Great Yarmouth in those days. Tea was served at little tables while the band played a succession of tuneful melodies or stirring military marches. Not far away the jetty and its seats were always crowded. Entrance to the jetty was free but a charge was made to go on the piers. It was all in the holiday mood but of a sedate, orderly, well-mannered era.

Our visits to Yarmouth usually ended with Mother and three tired little boys hurrying across the bridge to catch the train home. The shopping bags seemed heavy, we were all tired, tempers were frayed and we worried about which platform held our train as we didn't wish to go to Lowestoft or London by mistake! Had we lost the tickets?

Chuffing away in summer was interesting as we picked out familiar landmarks one by one. A short stop at Belton then on over Belton Common with its heather, bracken and silver birch trees which we knew so well from bird-nesting expeditions. During the 1914-18 War it had been a firing-range and training area and in our day the trenches and rifle butts still remained. Strangely, I did firing-practice at those butts, which were restored for the Second World War, just a few, short years later.

As the train slowed on its approach to St. Olaves station, we passed the famous asparagus bed on the left belonging to the stationmaster, Mr. Barker. It was his pride and joy! Behind it was the Post Office and shop kept by Mrs Cooper, her son Jack and Florrie her daughter. Cooper's home-made ice-cream was famous and people came from miles around to buy it! How we loved St. Olaves station – the station house, the goods siding, Mr. Barker in his immaculate uniform and his wife and their two little girls. Then there was Mr. Gale and Mr. Brown, the kings of the signal box and masters of the massive crossing gates and young Bertie Sharman just starting his career as booking clerk.

In winters of the 1920s our local train carriages, being very old fashioned with no toilets and no corridor, were unheated as well. We were delighted when the porters trundled out trolleys loaded with long cylinders of boiling hot water to place in each compartment to act as radiators and warm our ice-cold feet. Off the train would go and we would gaze out into the black winter evening, picking out the few lighted windows that broke the darkness as we passed. When we left the lights of the train at the station, how dark it seemed as we faced the long walk home. Torches were more than welcome, and better still someone to meet us with a lantern. Then it was home and bed, dreaming of our day out to Yarmouth. I can remember it still . . . .

Thankfully I don't recall any of our trips to Yarmouth ending like this!

*What
a day
I've had*

at Yarmouth

Postmark: 6.30 pm, 30 July, 1913
Great Yarmouth to Nottinghill Gate

Dear All,

What a day I've had! Am writing this from the sands at Yarmouth. This is one of the grandest places I have ever been to and I shall write and tell you all about it soon.

Love C.